FROM GARDEN TO GATEWAY

From the Garden of England to the Gateway to Europe…Kent's role has changed dramatically as a result of decisions taken during the 1980s. From a quiet county of hopfields and orchards to a pivotal role in Britain's new European setting. From a county "tucked away" beyond London to literally the fast lane – with new road and rail schemes, from the M25 to the High Speed Channel Link.

How will the county cope with its rapidly changing role?

FROM GARDEN TO GATEWAY is a photographic record of the rapid changes throughout the county of Kent as it "progresses" towards its new role as the Gateway to Europe.

How is the county coping with the difficult balancing act of accepting new economic opportunities while maintaining its traditional Garden of England role?

In response to invitations in local newspapers, photographs were submitted by people from every corner of the county depicting changes that "had either delighted or troubled them".

*   *   *

Perhaps somewhat concerning, the vast majority of participants illustrated examples of changes which they regretted.

Even more worrying is the rapidity of that change. Unlike many a nostalgic look at "the way things were" reflecting changes over many decades past, most of the photographs herein depicting scenes that have been, or about to be, lost forever, were submitted during a single two year period, 1990 and 1991.

British Library Cataloguing-in-Publication Data.
A catalogue record for this book is available from
the British Library.

FROM GARDEN TO GATEWAY

A photographic record of the changing face of Kent

Recorded by

THE PEOPLE OF KENT

Help us to continue to record the changes as the county "progresses" towards the Year 2000.

FROM GARDEN TO GATEWAY

Photographed by the people of Kent.

Compiled and written by Edward W Cookson.

First published in 1992 by

HEATHROW PUBLICATIONS
Palace Business Estate
Maidstone ME15 9XU

ISBN 1 874344 00 0

Research Assistant: S Mercy

Countryside Advisor: David Allford

Design: Geoff Denney, Terry Palmar
Phototypesetting: Type-O-Graphics, Maidstone
Printed and bound in England by Biddles Ltd

ACKNOWLEDGEMENTS

The publishers wish to thank all of the photographers who submitted ideas/entries; the Council for the Protection of Rural England (Kent Branch); the judges, Brenda Trench (KCC), Harry Lambert (Adscene), and David Puttnam; Neil Clements of Adscene Newspapers; and in particular John Gear and Roy Martin of Camera Gear, sponsors of the original competition.

While every effort has been taken to check, wherever possible, the background to changes suggested, the publishers are unable to accept responsibility for any errors in the individual examples submitted in good faith by members of the public. In some cases areas initially under threat, and later reprieved, have been retained. In such cases the concern caused to often vast numbers of the Kentish population is considered sufficient justification for inclusion.

Part of the proceeds from the sale of this book will be donated to charities concerned with protecting Kent's countryside.

CPRE (Kent)
Kent Trust for Nature Conservation
Kent Federation of Amenity Societies
National Trust "Enterprise Neptune"

Dedicated to the next generation of photographers of Kent.

Our disappearing world

A couple sip tea as they watch part of the Kent countryside being bulldozed into the 21st Century.

D.W. Clark's picture of the Channel Tunnel rail link terminal works at Cheriton demonstrates vividly how our county is being forced to yield to the pressures of progress.

This is the winning image in Focus on the Garden of England, a major environmental photographic competition run in Adscene during 1990/91.

Sponsored by Kent photographic equipment firm Camera Gear, it was organised by the Kent branch of the Council for the Protection of Rural England, and Kent County Council's Clean Kent Campaign.

Hundreds of amateur photographers were out and about in Kent during that period picturing subjects which reflected the environmental pressures faced by the Garden of England. It is their photographs which form the basis of this book. Together with further submissions from environmental organisations and local amenity groups across the county, they form a record of the changing face of the county as we "progress" towards the Year 2000.

THIS IS ONLY THE BEGINNING...

While there have been so many changes occurring in the past couple of years, 1992 represents only the start of things to come for Kent.

The Channel Tunnel rail link, new road schemes and expanded towns are planned for the rest of this decade. The publishers would like to invite you, no matter the quality of your camera, to continue to record changes.

Please send us photographs of scenes in Kent which you feel may be about to disappear. Further details are given on page 126.

KENT'S MANY CHANGING FACES

Kent – a county of hops and oasts, apples, marshes and meadows, rolling downs and white cliffs.

The early 90s have marked the end of many such Kentish scenes.

THE CHANGING FACE OF KENT

A record by Kentish people of the dramatic changes taking place now in the early nineties.

There follow over 180 examples of actual or potential changes within our county. Recorded by people from Dartford to Dover. Many are welcome examples, some not so welcome. Some represent major projects, others small local schemes.

Most have been taken over a relatively short two year timespan – emphasising the rapidity of change in our county.

Entries fall into the following six categories:

**AGRICULTURE
ONCE QUIET SPOTS CLOSE TO TOWN
IN TOWN
ON THE WATERFRONT
TRANSPORT INFRASTRUCTURE
MISCELLANY OF MASTS AND MINERALS**

R. Watkins (Romney Marsh)

Applications to develop an area do not always go ahead. For the purposes of our book, however, sites for which larger-scale proposals have been made, and which have caused public concern, are considered to be sufficiently "at risk" to merit inclusion, even where final planning permission has/may not be given.

Take for example the High Speed Rail Link. Four routes were originally considered – each causing great concern, many sleepless nights, plus the consequential blight for residents along its route. Pressures on the people of Kent are represented just as poignantly by plans, first mooted and later rejected, as those which eventually go ahead. We make no apologies for retaining such examples.

CONTENTS

THE CPRE
KENT'S COUNTRYSIDE CAMPAIGNERS

In a region so densely populated as the South East, our countryside, parks, commons and green spaces are vitally important.

And yet the threats are mounting – proposed new trunk roads, even bypasses bypassing bypasses, consequential development from the Channel Tunnel, the High Speed Link, infill on sports grounds, churchland, railway sidings.

Where will it all stop?

How can local opinion be marshalled?

Kent's countryside needs a strong, responsible voice.

CPRE provides such a voice. For over 60 years it has helped form much of today's legislation on green belts, national parks and countryside planning laws – never opposing progress, but always representing the English Countryside.

From its full title, Council for the Protection of Rural England, one could be forgiven for thinking that CPRE is some sort of official body. Rather it is an independent charity supported by around 50,000 concerned individuals, plus many local conservation groups. It maintains a London headquarters, and employs professional planners and lobbyists to campaign for the countryside through well informed, carefully researched arguments and briefings to Parliament and Local Government.

IN KENT

CPRE's Kent branch has been one of the fastest growing in recent years. The organisation continuously seeks to increase local membership. CPRE believes that when those individual voices are brought together they can have a powerful effect. Every new member will add strength to the growing voice of the Countryside.

PATRON: H. M. The Queen
PRESIDENT: David Puttnam
CHAIRMAN: David Astor

THE CPRE
CHANGING FACE OF KENT
PHOTO COMPETITION

Early in 1991, the main prizewinners in the Adscene/CPRE/KCC competition were invited to County Hall, Maidstone, to receive valuable photographic prizes kindly sponsored by the Camera Gear chain of Kent photographic shops.

The four main prizes were awarded for the photographs shown in this section.

The competition was open to photographers of all standards, no matter the sophistication of their equipment.

With this in mind, the judges awarded marks as much for content as for photographic expertise.

CRITERIA FOR JUDGING

● The photographs should represent some form of change, positive or negative, in the County of Kent.

● The photo should illustrate the impact upon the environment of present-day practices from good architectural design, to motorway planning, to illegal fly-tipping.

● The quality of the photographs should be assessed for composition and technique. However, leeway can be allowed for entries which meet criteria (1) and (2) above, and yet which, quite obviously, have been taken with inexpensive cameras.

JUDGES

CPRE	David Puttnam
KCC	Brenda Trench
Adscene	Harry Lambert
Camera Gear	John Gear

11

Three photographs judged worthy of prizes:

2ND PRIZE. Richborough Power Station.
Bob Woodward (Broadstairs)

3RD PRIZE. M20 Motorway Works.
Mrs R King (Lenham)

4TH PRIZE. Channel Tunnel Site at
Night. Paul Richardson (Deal)

An imaginative contrast between power
generation, old and new, finely
photographed; a new road gives the old
roadsign an ironic twist; and a dramatic
night-time shot of Channel Tunnel works
at Shakespeare Cliff.

JUDGES' FIRST CHOICE

Channel Tunnel Railway Terminal, Cheriton.
Dan Clark (Herne Bay)

A scene of devastation covering a vast area
(about half of this photograph) – but the
stretch of concrete between the Downs
and the Channel depicted here is but a
"taste" of the total effect on this
once beautiful region, as you will see on
the next two pages.

Channel Tunnel Site. Panorama D W Clark (Herne Bay)

Throughout the book, the
designation <s> is used to indicate
other photographs shortlisted by the
judges.

Help us to continue to record the changes. Details page 126.

AGRICULTURE

CEP, CAP, GATT, FEOGA and MacSharry…a plethora of policies and proposals from both Brussels and Westminster have faced Kent's farmers over the past few years.

AHDS, AHGS, HLCA…incentives to produce more, incentives to produce less. To set-aside, to remove hedges, to plant hedges. Inorganic or organic? Intensification, extensification, or diversification? And the designations – AONBs and SSSIs; LFAs, ESFAs, UFFAs and MUAs.

Confused? It's no wonder that the agricultural community often finds it hard to know which way to turn under a spate of impositions and directives. And how can we expect the countryside to be totally unaffected by this state of flux?

Some Kentish farming communities go back centuries – could the eighties have marked an irreversible turning point?

AGRICULTURAL BUILDINGS

Yesterday the "Darling Buds of May". Nowadays many farm settings are no longer quite so "perfick".
Paul Harvey (Horsmonden) <s>

Old barns. "So what?" some might ask of such dereliction. Yet for centuries, these buildings have been in productive agricultural use. Whether well-converted or left to decay, their demise as farm buildings reflects the pressures on the agricultural way of life.

Examples submitted of barns.

Right: At Ebbsfleet near Richborough. J Burgess

Below: Near Ulcombe. Mrs Micklewright (Sittingbourne)

Opposite page

Above: Mark Howard (Hawkinge)

Below: Colin Holloway (Tunbridge Wells)

The old barn at Sole, Gravesend. *Top* in 1988, *bottom* in
1990. K L Boxall (Meopham) <s>

Above right: Old Oasts near Ashford.
'Ripe for development?' asks
Mrs Alder (Singleton)

Below right: New Oasts? Site of old
agricultural premises, Oad Street.
K W R Washford (Sittingbourne)

FRUITS OF THE GARDEN – HOPFIELDS

Hopfields...
Paul Harvey, Horsmonden, poses
the question how long will these
scenes last with current changes to
traditional brewing methods?

– ORCHARDS

"End of another orchard"
This makes about seven in the Little Barton area reports
William Harvey (Canterbury)

Left: Orchard in line of Northern Ring Road. Colin Pillen
(Rochester)

Above: The sign near Ashford says it all.

Above: Apple orchards in one of Ashford's new housing zones. Suggested by Shirley Moorhead (Ashford)

Below: How will proposals to replace this orchard with a skislope/golf complex, carparks and access roads affect this beautiful valley, near Canterbury?

Above: Traditional apple stock, fast disappearing. R Baxter
(Wye)

Below: A pleasant approach to Bearsted's village church –
housing has been proposed for orchards to the right.
C Dunn (Bearsted)

Hedgerow losses, Little Chart.
In this case, not for arable farming,
but to make way for the M20.
Tony Richardson (Maidstone)

"Hedgerows rich in wildlife and some more than 1000 years old. Between 1984 and 1990, 53,000 miles (24% of total) were grubbed out, lost to intensive farming."
From The Times, May 1992

Grazing land, Chattenden, scheduled for housing
development. Colin Pillen (Rochester)

DIVERSIFICATION

With agriculture under pressure, what alternative sources of income can a farmer seek? Is agriculture in Kent fast polarising into two distinct camps – the major commercial concerns and part-time farming? In marginal areas, especially close to London, farmers can find it much more attractive to sell their land for alternative developments. That's all very well. But, having sold up, after a lifetime (maybe generations) of country living, where do Kentish farming families re-establish their roots?

Right: Hewitt's Farm, Orpington. Following construction of the M25, extensive shopping developments were proposed, testing Green Belt policies to the full.

What the…?

Horsiculture – where large fields are split into smaller lots – has become a common feature in some parts.
C Hancock (Coulsden)

Imagine these pages in colour. (Reproduced on cover).

From traditional to chemical and back to organic farming as reflected by the re-establishment of fields of poppies.

Examples submitted included:

Left: Alkham Valley. Michael Twinn (Thornaby) <s>

Below right: By the A249 at Stockbury. D Woodhouse (Sittingbourne)

Below left: And red is not the only bright colour to appear in recent years. Rape fields, Lower Rainham Road. J Cossan.

Opposite page: Stubble burning now banned. Oliver Reeves (Ashford)

SET ASIDE A BARN
"Farm building conversions into dwelling houses could see the replacement in the farmyard of the farmworker's bicycle by the middle class Mercedes" fears H S Buckhurst (Canterbury) <s>

Over 5% of Kent's orchards – some 780h – were lost between 1989 and 1991.

ONCE QUIET SPOTS CLOSE TO TOWN

So many contributors submitted photographs of favourite spots on the outskirts of town, which they fear could soon be despoilt – well-loved walks, perhaps known only to locals, places for a picnic, or a quiet evening stroll with the dog.

Most areas have such beauty spots just a few minutes walk away. But are they disappearing fast as new estates extend town boundaries ever further from the centre…as new road schemes, often built to relieve the High Street, noisily skirt the fringes? When bypasses become the new boundaries, could many Kent towns be left with a virtually impassible swathe of concrete, replacing once quiet pathways into the countryside by a corridor of noise?

A Challenge

Have we all but lost these quiet spots close to town? Now, here's a challenge to anyone who lives in any reasonably-sized town in Kent. Can you nominate your "special place". Perhaps by a pool or river, maybe with a view. No more than a "dogswalk" away from home, where you can still enjoy peace and quiet, away from traffic noise?

Send us your nomination with the coupon on page 127 and you could win £250 for yourself and a charity.

A place of peace and quiet, natural beauty, Oare, Faversham.

Once hidden, now "opened up" following the building of the Western Relief Road. Marilyn Spice (Ashford) <s>

Above: Youth hostels.
After 45 years of providing low-cost accommodation for hikers, the hostel at Crockham Hill has closed. Could this be the result of a new commercial approach somewhat removed from the association's original ideals? Suggested by K. Reynolds (Crockham Hill).

CHANGED PRIORITIES

For centuries, the people of Sevington could walk safely to church. However, now it seems we have different priorities – the village divided by Ashford's new southern orbital ring road *(above)*.

A quiet village, Sevington even retains its old, red telephone box. (We've lost many such boxes since 1990.)

Bad medicine never comes in single doses. Perhaps to help pay for the road through Sevington, the local authorities, it seems, needed to totally swamp the village with housing and hypermarkets. Orbital roads such as Ashford's have already altered beyond recognition villages such as Sevington.

Suggested by Shirley Moorhead (Ashford)

You could once look out across fields over Herne Bay to the distant sea (*left*) from this vantage point in Bullockstone Road. The new track in the foreground and telephone pole (*below*) mark the end of this viewpoint and the onset of a new housing estate. Richard Mackenzie (Herne Bay)

"Tranquility". But for how long? Heidi and Mrs Russell (Whitfield, Dover)

Above: Chilmington Farm in route of Ashford Ring Road.

What has happened to Sevington (page 38) is due to happen to Chilmington in the very near future. Again, much "consequential" development including thousands of houses, is planned for this quiet meadowland.

Suggested by Shirley Moorhead (Ashford)

Playing fields on the edge of Borough Green. Soon to be
closely "clipped" by the town's new by-pass.

A proposed skislope of massive proportions could spoil
this skyline forever. Esther David (The Whitstable
Society)

OUT OF SIGHT...

A quiet little place just off the beaten track.
Out-of-sight can attract "out-of-mind" fly tippers.

Top left: Pleasant country walk, Shadoxhurst, fast
becoming a dumping ground. A S Jackson (Ashford)

Top right: Disused railway line, Dartford, by Chris Penny
(Dartford) <s>

Bottom left: Fly tipping in Barming Woods. Michael Tester
(Maidstone) <s>

Bottom right: Shawstead Road, Lordswood by John Hall
(Chatham) <s>

In 1990, it was estimated that Kent's existing waste tips would be full within 2/3 years.

CAR SCARS

Scars on the countryside from the all too frequent practice
of dumping old vehicles.

Illustrated in photographs by

Top left: Kingsdown Beach, Paul Richardson (Deal)

Centre left: ZsuZsi Brand (Monkton)

Bottom left: Romney Marsh, Oliver Reeves (Ashford)

Above: K L Boxall (Meopham) <s>

Leybourne Woods – a dappled wonderland of woods and streams, clearings and signs of play. Possibly in line of Leybourne bypass. Suggested by Mrs Christopherson (Ryarsh)

IN TOWN

New nineties shopping centres…or a preference for the traditional? Whatever your taste, there are many signs of change taking place in our town centres. We have space for just a small selection including a few pointers to ways in which certain traditions, such as town markets, are beginning to succumb to "progress".

This section more than any other, allowed contributors to be positive. There are many good things planned for our towns.

Two examples from Mrs Doreen Coppin's interesting collection of scenes from the late eighties, and how they look today.

Alongside the traditional lines of County Hall, the new Municipal Insurance Building, Maidstone.

Top: Science Parks – high quality commercial developments are planned for West Malling (see page 110), Ashford (pictured), and within the East Thames corridor.

Bottom: Hotels – several very large hotels sprang up during 1990/91. Two or three years ago, the oast in the background looked out over open countryside.

Top: In the home video age, local cinemas are in decline, as illustrated by the former Herne Bay Classic. B Smith (Herne Bay)

Below: The town centre cinema, it is sometimes said, lost out to television. In 1991, not even the TV stations are safe. TVS provided an excellent service to Kent, often with that 'local' feel. To date, the decision to axe it makes little sense on any level. Will we notice the change when it's gone?

Churches and church halls, now redundant *(top and centre)*. But a new church for Ashford *(bottom)*.

Top: St Nicholas's Church Hall, Sevenoaks. A single building perhaps to be replaced by flats and six houses. Eric Keys (Sevenoaks Society)

INFILL KILLS

Infill can kill a neighbourhood. When single plots, each with a large house and garden, are redeveloped as mini-estates – they change dramatically the character of a street, raising housing densities, traffic flows etc. Isn't there a case for less infilling? Once a residential area has already been planned at a certain density, then why not let it be?

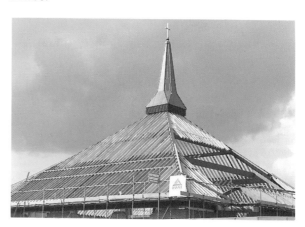

Centre: Christ Church, Tunbridge Wells. Martin Cullingford (Tunbridge Wells)

Below: Mike Stampton (Dover)

MARKET FORCES

Markets, a centuries-old tradition, perhaps lost forever to "market forces" of the past decade.

Top: Sevenoaks market, Eric Keys (Sevenoaks Society)

Below: Ashford market, suggested by Shirley Moorhead (Ashford)

Sports centres, particularly those in town centres, have been under considerable redevelopment pressure lately. Non-league clubs without the clout of their Football league cousins – and yet with comparable sized pitches – are especially vulnerable.

Above: Sittingbourne market, plus the adjacent football ground, site of a planned supermarket. K Washford (Sittingbourne) <s>

Right: A new "Temple to Self Assembly" to replace Maidstone FC's old ground. Now the team is forced to play well over a Stone's throw away from the town it represents.

Above: The old bus station Sevenoaks,
soon to be developed.

Below: Blighs Meadow, Sevenoaks, a
site of great debate.

Both submitted by Eric Keys
(Sevenoaks Society)

A new international station for Ashford will replace its traditional lines. Suggested by Shirley Moorhead (Ashford)

Upsetting to the Greens? And let's not forget the root crops. Maidstone allotments allotted new roundabout.

Carrs Corner. A new junction for this attractive feature of Tunbridge Wells. Martin Cullingford (TW Civic Society)

PARKS

Right: Proposed road improvements/ roundabout will slice into Dunloran Park, Tunbridge Wells.
Martin Cullingford (Tunbridge Wells Civic Society)

Vine Paddocks, by Knole Park. Proposed housing area.
The Sevenoaks Western Relief Road could clip the park.
Eric Keys (Sevenoaks Society)

Stangrove Park, Edenbridge.
Site of proposed relief road
(First Edenbridge Cub Scouts) <s>

Juggernauts could soon pass
by this children's play area, and by the
park's pond which contains rare
newts (on right of top photo).
(Edenbridge Residents' Association)

Plea of nature? Shadows
outline the new road's route – cast by
mature trees in its path.

INSTITUTIONS: HOSPITALS

Many institutional buildings such as hospitals, in extensive grounds, and schools with playing fields can be tempting development prospects for local authorities.

The grounds of Darenth Park Hospital – a new "village" of 900 houses is proposed for this area of Green Belt. Suggested by George Allan (Dartford)

SCHOOLS

Could we be about to lose the village school – arguably the heart of the village community – in many parts of Kent? In Edenbridge, rationalisation has resulted in the closure of the town's well-loved Middle School (EMS) – a thriving school into which the smaller village schools "feed". Although it had a strong school roll plus one of the best inspectors' reports in the county, EMS's closure (probably for housing development) will lead to great pressure on the area's village schools, such as Marsh Green (above).

ON THE WATERFRONT

Surrounded on three sides by the sea and crisscrossed by rivers, water is one of the County's key assets for recreation and tourism. But could there already be disturbing signs of troubled waters?

An expanding population, increased extraction, for private, public and recreational uses, golfcourses in particular, a yearning to redevelop some of our watersides as private marinas – and added to such pressures, several years of low rainfall.

What changes will the 1990s bring to Kent on the water "front"?

RIVERS

Greenhouse effect. Or just two years of drought. Several rivers within Kent now dry up completely at certain times of the year.

Top: The Darent, Horton Kirby, in 1990 (left) – freeflowing and "teeming with fish." *Right:* In the Summer of 1991. Mrs C. Jenner (Erith)

Below: The River Nailbourne, Bourne Park, Bridge, 1990. "Could the floods of 1988/89 be the last real flow of this river?" asks H.J. Buckhurst (Canterbury)

Above and below: Soon to change? The Great Stour
meanders through a designated housing area.
Suggested by Shirley Moorhead (Ashford)

Photograph page 59: F. W. Crow
(Strood).

"SITE FOR SORE EYES"
How the people of Edenbridge lost sight of the Eden Bridge and gained a site for "sore eyes".

In 1989, a bend in the River Eden...

...leading to the Great Stone Bridge that gave Edenbridge its name.

Today…

…a new bridge, as yet going nowhere.

The trees have made way for a new access/relief road. Need they have been felled at all? (Submitted by Edenbridge Residents' Association)

Above: Stoneham Lock, Yalding. On a bend in the River Medway, surrounded by open countryside. A favourite picnic spot for many locals now to be a leisure development. Original proposal, since tempered, included an 80 room hotel, marina, chalets and caravan site, riding stables. Suggested by E. Melling (Maidstone)

Below: The medieval stone bridge at Fordwich has been replaced by a new one of brick. The road sign says it all.

RESERVOIRS

Above: Doomed cottage in the valley? Possibly, if the proposed Broad Oak Reservoir goes ahead. <s>

Left: Bridge Under Troubled Water, also threatened by the Broad Oak Reservoir. I Bolton (Canterbury)

The average demand for water rose by 1½% pa in the years to 1988.

KENT'S ESTUARIES AND HARBOURS

Reflections of the past. J. Cossan (Rainham) <s>

Restoring an old industry.
Dolphin Barge Yard, Sittingbourne.
John Wallis (Chatham)

The Medway.
For centuries people have been
able to stroll along its banks
"watching the ships sail by".

Above and right: The Strand,
Gillingham. A pleasant corridor of
green – soon to be swamped by the
Northern Link Road. Suggested by
David Murr (Gillingham)

Allotments in route of Gillingham
Northern Link Road. Suggested by
David Murr (Gillingham)

Similarly in Maidstone, the
Medway, perhaps the town's
greatest asset, is flanked by noisy
dual carriageways, soon to be
extended beyond the distant
buildings.

North Kent Marshes – stretching in a continuous belt from Gravesend to Whitstable – this internationally important breeding ground for birds, offers a feeling of remoteness unusual in the South East. Most of this area is within the East Thames Corridor growth area. Parts are threatened by mineral extraction and road schemes.

The photo shows Oare Marshes, courtesy Faversham News.

Above: Sheppey's wetlands seemingly stretch
undisturbed. Large housing schemes are planned for the
island. R Baxter (Wye)

Below: On the banks of the Medway, the Merchant Navy
College lies empty. Suggested by George Allan (Dartford)

FERRIES

The pre-Channel Tunnel days have proven to be a testing and challenging time for Kent's ferry operators.

Services that had seemed to be "permanent fixtures" are undergoing a major revolution.

Hovercraft services have been curtailed but we now have the new and exciting SeaCat.

Routes have had to close – but new Super Ferries are "on the horizon".

Right: The now derelict immigration buildings at Pegwell Hoverport, a former natural beauty spot, an attraction to visitors.

This development testifies to the neglect which may have contributed to a fall in visitors to East Kent.
C Parker (Ramsgate)

Below: External view. Ian Bowman (Ramsgate)

Top: In 1991, the Folkestone to Boulogne route was closed...after 150 years. No more do the Horsa and Hengist (photo courtesy Sealink Stena line) sail out of Folkestone.

Centre: Hovercraft "Princess Anne" leaving Dover Hoverport. F Jepson (Deal)

Below: A new sight in Folkestone and Dover – the record-breaking Hoverspeed SeaCat (courtesy Sea Containers Ltd).

Queen Elizabeth II bridge – a majestic new northern
gateway into the county. An unusual view taken from the
water by Capt W T Richardson.

TRANSPORT

No other category brought quite the same response as transport. In most, we had examples of changes people welcomed. Transport changes seemed to appall most of our participants. One wonders why the planners/politicians are so obsessed with new roads. Even though, when completed, roads are on the whole very well landscaped, you cannot hide the noise they generate. You cannot rejoin the communities they divide. You can never re-create the countryside they destroy. From the Northern Ring Road to the new coastal trunk road, Kent is fast becoming encircled in concrete.

MOTORWAY
MADNESS?

Fast becoming a development cliché
in Kent. Contractors' crosses *(above)*
plus the monolitic slabs mockingly
mark the demise of this tract of quiet
countryside beneath the Downs
near Harrietsham. Mrs R King
(Lenham)

The M20 extension between Maidstone and Ashford was captured by many competitors.

Top left: From Meadows to Motorways. From fresh air to carbon monoxide. T W Billington (Maidstone) who also provided the photo on page 75. <s>

Top right: On the Road to Ruin. A country lane (no more) near Lenham. Gloria Lavender (Ashford)

Bottom: Lone Tree. D A and J A Woodhouse (Sittingbourne) <s>

Top: Contractors clear the woods on the skyline, seen from the A20 near Leeds Castle.

Below: Today juggernauts dominate the skyline, following construction of the embankment for the M20. Note the traffic in this area on the A20 seems as busy as ever. T Palmar (Maidstone)

Hollingbourne

Top left and centre: An avenue of horse chestnuts led to this quiet village by the North Downs. J Garnham Wright (Hollingbourne)

Below and top right: The same two scenes, respectively, today. No longer an avenue, a single beech survived the M20 blitz. And across this scene – the possible route of the High Speed Rail Link (see page 105).

Right: As if a new motorway and railway aren't enough. Why not site a new motorway service station next to the village? These fields, adjacent to a wood of special wildlife interest, were chosen, we understand, rather than a nearby derelict industrial site. Ironically, the area's seemingly protected status – with a longstanding presumption against development – made it less costly for the DoT to purchase than the designated commercial site. Until the DoT learns to put a price on "our priceless" countryside, such anomalies will surely continue.

On the Surrey/Kent border, "the largest project on the motorway network". That's how Roadchef describe their new M25 service station. Why so large? And why in such an environmentally sensitive area at the foot of the North Downs? (Indeed, our ancestors might ask, why at all was the M25, below right, sited in one of the most beautiful parts of southern England?)

Have you a favourite spot? Win £250 – page 127.

M20 WIDENING

They are moving "mountains" around Maidstone
(well hillsides and the hundreds of trees that line
them). The crooked fence and Cobtree Museum
sign used to nestle amid woods on the hillside.
Today they lie on the very edge.

THE THANET WAY

A dangerous road, dualled. But was it necessary to extend it "off-line" through beautiful countryside – another example of a bypass to bypass a bypass? And why was it necessary to infill the surrounding fields with a plethora of superstores? These will surely attract more traffic to the route, and will undermine established towncentre stores nearby.

Top: Proposed route of Thanet Way from Shrubb Hill. Suggested by Elizabethan Walker (Chestfield)

Right: "This house lay on the corner of a country lane. Now it may be demolished for a superstore car park," reports R. Mackenzie (Herne Bay).

NORTHERN LINK

Will the Northern Link relieve or devastate the
Medway towns? We have already seen, on page 69,
its stranglehold on the Strand. It will also pass
through meadows and marshland, through
playing fields and pastures.

CHANNEL TUNNEL

The Channel Tunnel is arguably one of the greatest civil engineering feats ever undertaken. Could it also prove to be one of the greatest excuses for consequential development within the county of Kent? Its dendritic, fickle fingers will stretch far and wide across the South East. For many years to come environmentally damaging road schemes will find justification in that they "serve the Channel Tunnel". Its high profile has seemingly been used to wreak a level of destruction on the county of Kent that few planners would have countenanced in the past. Has the European dimension taken precedence over local feelings?

There was a certain inevitability about the M20 extension to Folkestone. But that was only the beginning. Each of the new schemes shown here will follow. Many pass through some of the most sensitive parts of the South East.

Holywell and Sugarloaf Hill before and during construction. It is hoped that much of this area will be reinstated once the M20 has been extended across it. But will it ever again be so quiet? Rob Cameron (Wye)

The countryside around Folkestone used to be a patchwork of rolling hills, woods and streams.

Left top: Former view from Cheriton Hill with its distinctive channels.

Left below: Biggins Wood, with channels in foreground.

Right top and below: Former views from base of Cheriton Hill. On the skyline stands Cherry Garden Hill just north of Biggins Wood. John and Irene Palmer (Orpington)

View from opposite side of Cherry Garden Hill showing
Biggins Wood.

Top: John & Irene Palmer's earlier view.

Below: Rob Cameron's 1990 photograph.

Between the Chunnel and the deep blue sea.

What future for Folkestone and Cheriton as quiet seaside towns hemmed in by the M20?

Above: How this area used to look. John & Irene Palmer (Orpington)

An updated version of Dan Clark's panorama of the Channel Tunnel Terminal. See page 15. Dan Clark (Herne Bay)

The White Cliffs around Dover. Not merely environmentally superb, but a symbol of British independence for 1000 years. They wouldn't...

Cliffs around St Margarets Bay. Frank Jepson (Deal)

...They have!!

Hacked out of the chalk, you can see the foundations for
the A20/M20 extension, photographed by F Jepson (Deal)
cutting across the cliffs to the West of Dover.

There is a certain irony in the M20/A20 across the White Cliffs. It has been argued that Dover needs better communications within the motorway network, to redress the perceived imbalance to the town's trade when it *loses cross-channel traffic* to the Tunnel. In other words, a reduction in traffic will lead to more roads.

Shakespeare Cliffs
Above: Martin Trelawny
Below: Frank Jepson (Deal)

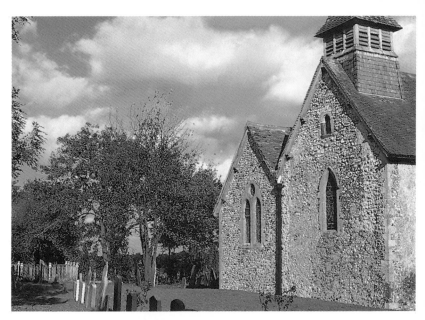

DOVER – *continued*

The loss of headland behind Shakespeare Cliffs is only the beginning.

"A collar of concrete is planned for this historic town," reports Jim Davis (Dover). His examples include links around Dover to the M20 and the M2.

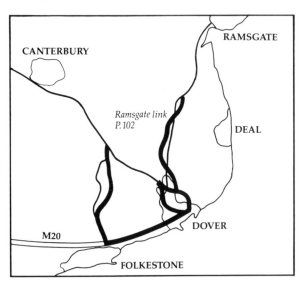

Ramsgate link P.102

To the East of Dover
The quiet churchyard at Church Whitfield could overlook the proposed Whitfield bypass *(top)*. It will pass through this area of open fields and country lanes *(centre)*, including Eastling Woods to the right of this photograph.

To the West of Dover
An extended A2 (T) will bypass Denton and Wooton close to Denton churchyard *(below)*.

Hawkinge Airfield lies in the path of the "concrete collar". The airfield, of "Battle of Britain" significance, could face its final battle soon. Future historians will surely demand to know why one of the most historic sites from World War II was sacrificed for Chunnel Traffic.

West of Dover, the A20 will be re-routed through the Alkham Valley. Leonard Green (Hawkinge)

Left: In 1989.

Above: In 1992.

The fickle fingers will stretch ever further, ever wider...

A new trunk road will blast its way North-South to meet the Ashford International rail terminal.

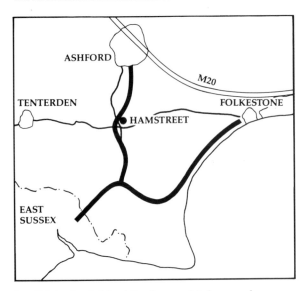

It will join the Ashford Southern orbital somewhere near Sevington (see page 38).

To the South it will cut across the Apsley Wood Valley *(top)*. And will it make a real pig's ear of the peaceful pastures around Ham Street?

The A20/M20 will be linked into the Honiton to Folkestone A27/M27 route – a new South coast trunk road, which some argue the DoT has built by stealth, by constructing one bypass after another – a concrete coastal strip from Devon to Dover.

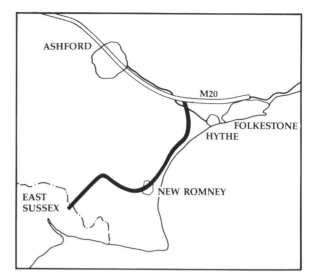

The major link will cross Romney Marsh and the Military Canal *(top)* to climb the Downs near Lympne Castle *(bottom)* before joining the A20/M20 near Folkestone. Tony Briggs (New Romney)

Over the Military Canal, the new
road will climb the Downs.
Suggested by David Allford.

The Dover "dendrites" creep North. Improved links will be needed from Thanet to the Docks, passing through woods at Eastry (*top*) and skirting Tilmanstone (*below*).

Below: In the proposed route of Tilmanstone bypass. Suggested by Margaret Robson (Tilmanstone)

Ramsgate. What effect will the Tunnel have on the port? It is claimed that better access will help the port compete. A new access road is planned.

But isn't this yet another example of roadbuilding to redress a perceived reduction in traffic due to competition. Such schemes are suggested not *to meet* increased traffic but *to bring about* an increase in traffic. (See page 95)

This damaging proposal could ruin the chalk cliffs west of Pegwell Bay plus adjacent beaches and the River Stour wildfowl reserve.

Top: Richard Tait (Pegwell and District Association)

Below: Ian Bowman (Ramsgate)

RAIL LINKS

But let's not get completely carried away by road
schemes. Spare a thought for the railways. And
many a concerned thought kept many a Kentish
Man awake at nights, pondering which of the
original four routes of the High Speed Link, (plus
two or three freight lines) would be chosen by BR.
Hopefully, the latest Ove Arup will be the best
environmentally…

Along the High Speed Link several new stations
have been proposed including ones at Ashford,
Maidstone Parkway and on the M25 near Dartford
(a possible recipe for motorway chaos). How can
this be a fast, through link to the Continent, if the
train stops at new stations every ten minutes?

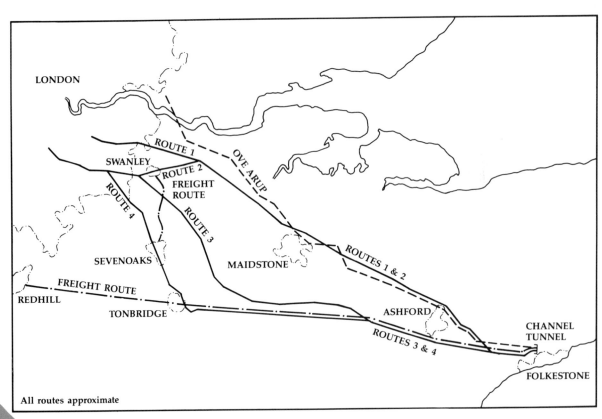

BR first suggested four routes to the south of London
with *additional* freight routes.

Two short years – most of
the changes depicted here
are from 1990/91.

Top: Cows graze next to the new M20 extension and on, possibly, the route of the High Speed Rail Link. Suggested by Elizabeth Melling (Maidstone)

Below: From Bluebell Hill picnic site, valley under threat from High Speed Rail Link. Pamela Mannering (Chatham)

Finally, the upgrading of existing lines will also have its effects.

Top: The Orient Express evokes thoughts of a quieter, relaxed age. A S Child (Ashford) fears that this cottage may be lost in the widening of the stretch of track between Folkestone and Ashford. <s>

Below: International Freight demands fast through routes to the continent unhindered by "leaves on the line". One BR answer – a tree felling programme that seemingly could cost the South East hundreds of thousands of trees.

MISCELLANEOUS CONTRIBUTIONS – FROM MASTS TO MINERALS

Let's end on a quieter note. Finally, a miscellany of subjects.

Signs, storms, airfields…and coalfields.

Mining industry contraction, mineral extraction. And finally, a tilt at windmills – a peaceful signoff or a reminder that "the inevitable" can be challenged.

SIGNS

A sign of these changing times, or…a time of changing signs

Clear road signs are of course paramount on trunk roads and motorways – but on country lanes, some might beg to differ. Since 1989, the KCC have substituted the majority of our charming country signposts, of wood or metal, by "plastic-looking" replacements which are generally more obtrusive and often lacking in character.

The old signs somehow helped differentiate between the fast lane and the country lane – best "pottered" along on tractor, horseback, bike or foot. The new signs are very clear especially for drivers in a hurry. But, in our villages, shouldn't we be calming traffic, rather than giving extra encouragement to speed?

STORMS

No catalogue of change either side of 1990 would be complete without some mention of the Great Storms of 1987 and 1990. Nearly 2 million trees were estimated to have fallen in Kent. We received many storm photographs. However, mindful of other excellent and comprehensive studies on this theme, in particular those of Bob Ogley, we have limited our selection to just one "hopeful" image.

"Natural disaster, natural recovery" by John Wood (Herne Bay) illustrates a Canterbury sculpture – carved from a tree felled in the 1987 storm.

AIRFIELDS

Kent was in the forefront of the Battle of Britain – in the past two years airfields, which have endured since the war, have "fallen" to the attraction of alternative developments. Could the era of Airshows be over – West Malling (1991) and Biggin Hill (1992) have seen their last public flypasts. See also the Hawkinge Airfield example on page 97. Suggested by T Palmar (Maidstone)

COALFIELDS

The Kent Coalfields are all but gone. Snowdown Colliery. As it was (*left*) and today (*top right*). William Harvey (Canterbury)

Bottom right: "And then there were none", Betteshanger Colliery. P Mackay (Deal)

Photograph page 107: As former pit towers go, new mobile communications towers appear. One estimate suggests that the countryside could be covered by a matrix of such masts, one mile apart. C Hancock (Coulsden)

MINERALS

Top: View from Bluebell Hill Picnic Site. New chalk-pit being dug out for cement works in Snodland.
John Mannering (Chatham)

Below: There are proposals to extract gravel from various sites across Kent including this unusual dry valley at Highstead (*right*) and beyond the bridge at Chartham Hatch (*left*).
Suggested by Bob Baxter (Wye).

WINDMILLS

Wind Power, past and present, seemed to catch the
imagination of many of our participants.

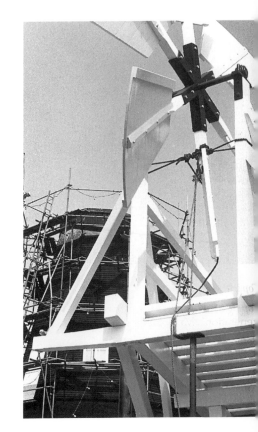

Top left: P M Castle

Top right: "Cleaner, safer power generation". Mr Goldstone (Minster)

Bottom left: Sarre Mill. Sue White (Charlton)

Bottom right: "Power need not corrupt". A E Crocker (Minster)

Experimental wind turbine, Richborough.
2nd prize winner
Bob Woodward (Broadstairs)

Our "tilt" at windmills may be an
appropriately peaceful reminder of more
leisurely times with which to end this
selection of photographs. We thank all of
our photographers including the many for
whose work we were unable to find space.

Your efforts are much appreciated, as is
your concern in Kent's environment. We
hope that you will continue to send us
contributions on the same theme of change
in Kent. We, in turn, will endeavour to
continue to publish the best examples in
future works.

The selection of over 200 photos is just a small fraction of the thousands we could have included – thousands of examples of changes mainly to the Kent countryside and within our historic towns…

…From Garden to Gateway

Could Kent's destiny have been determined in just three or four short years?

HOW THE SOUTH-EAST COULD CONTINUE TO CHANGE

The following schemes have been discussed for the South-East and Kent in particular.

MOTORWAYS/TRUNK ROADS

A M25 expansion with "feeder" lanes alongside the existing motorway – a total of 14 lanes of traffic through the Green Belt.

B An outer orbital beyond the M25, by linking existing and proposed bypasses in the Home Counties. But could this new trunk road, which passes close to the Ashdown Forest, lead to new developments all along its route?

C A Hampshire to Ashford link across the Weald.

D Medway towns Northern relief road.

E Over fifty new bypasses/ring roads or improved stretches (eg by widening) of existing routes are planned by the KCC.

F Various road schemes related to the Channel Tunnel, see pages 87 to 99.

EAST THAMES CORRIDOR

G A possibly commendable initiative to enhance the environment of North Kent by encouraging the redevelopment of under used and derelict land. However, new development must respect the Green Belt and sensitive wildlife areas such as the North Kent marshes. The Corridor stretches from Docklands along both banks of the Thames to Sittingbourne in Kent and Southend in Essex.

RAILWAYS

H The High Speed Link and Channel freight lines.

I An extended North Kent line.

HOUSING

J Land supply for nearly 60,000 new completions has been proposed for the current decade including:

Ashford	10,000 new houses
Maidstone	7,000 new houses
North Kent/Medway	16,000 new houses
Sevenoaks/Tonbridge/ Tunbridge Wells	6,000 new houses
Canterbury/Herne Bay	4,000 new houses
Thanet	4,000 new houses
Dover	4,000 new houses
Folkestone/Romney Marsh	4,000 new houses
Dartford	5,000 new houses

AIRPORTS

K The expansion of aviation at Lydd and Manston is to be considered.

How the South East looks now

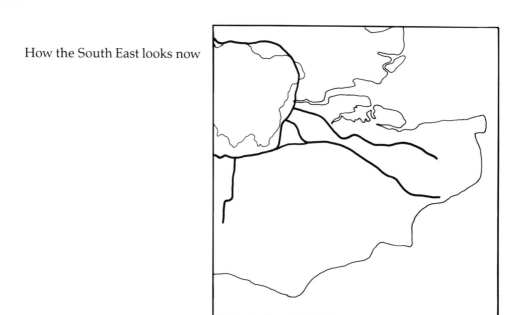

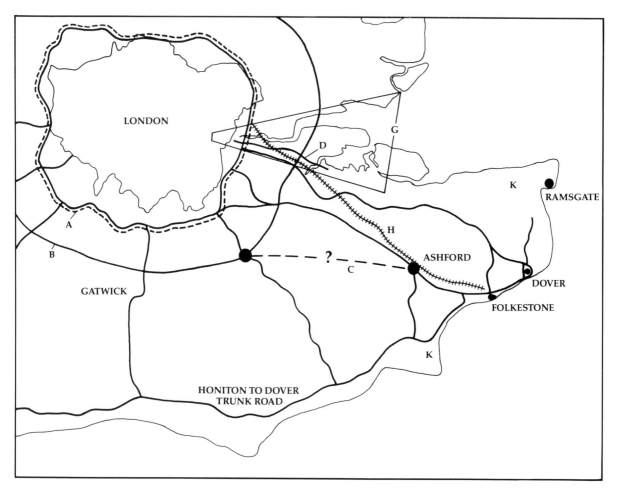

How the South East might look at the end of the decade.

THE SCALE AND PACE OF CHANGE ...

What can I possibly do...to influence the pace and scale of change?

How many times do you hear from friends and neighbours "they are spoiling this or that particular area with their developments", or "...it's pure greed that makes them cram in so many cheap houses, rather than an interest in the local community". And from official bodies; "it's a Department of Transport scheme, of national importance", ..."there are too many *NIMBY*'s concerned with their own 'backyard' interests rather than the good of the whole area".

When it comes to planning, it often seems that there are two definite camps – them and us. They want to change things, we want to be left in peace.

But perhaps the most telling comment so widely and often despairingly voiced is:

"What can we as individuals do about it, when faced with official government bodies or 'big business' interests?"

Both where necessary can afford to employ the best lawyers and planning experts to "push" through their schemes, the former, incidentally, with our money.

GET ORGANISED

The answer is that there is quite a lot you can do. Believe it or not, the planning system is one of the most democratic we enjoy. If you have a viewpoint, then usually the system will consider it, especially where local/county schemes are under debate.

But it's no use waiting until final decisions are taken and then complaining that they are wrong. You need to become involved as soon as possible at the formative stage. In Kent, you can do this in several ways, either individually or by joining and supporting one or more organised groups in the county.

LOCAL GROUPS

Most towns in Kent have a local amenity society or residents' group. You can obtain their address from your library or council offices or through an umbrella organisation such as the Kent Federation of Amenity Societies, KFAS – details on page 125.

Through them you can meet like-minded individuals, learn of planning applications well in advance and provide a joint case to the authorities on changes within your town that you would welcome, as well as those you don't agree with.

If you haven't a local group – then why not start one. The Civic Trust (telephone 071-930 0914) provide an excellent publication on how to get started.

Council for the Protection of Rural England

COUNTRYSIDE, COUNTYWIDE

If you have a "global view", and are concerned by what is happening, or could happen, to Kent's countryside as a whole, then why not join the CPRE – one of the most effective organisations in putting across the views of concerned individuals to planners and politicians...at their level.

Despite its full title, the Council for the Protection of Rural England, which can make it sound like some sort of official body, the CPRE is in fact an environmental charity – of very long-standing – supported almost entirely by contributions and membership fees, and is open to everyone with a love of and concern for the English countryside.

Professional Planners...on your side

As individuals, we may know what we would like to see happen, but how do we express it when faced by official documents, often bogged down in planning jargon. "What is the right way to put my case across? Will I look silly, or self-interested if I object to that?" If you've ever felt this way, then despair no more. Join the CPRE.

The CPRE uses members' donations to employ highly professional planners and lobbyists to meet with local authorities and government ministers to discuss the effects of their policies on the English countryside. Whenever a big road scheme, or an expanded town is mooted, the CPRE is often there to present the case for the countryside, rarely objecting just for the sake of it, often suggesting alternative ways of meeting the housing/transport objectives.

A well-respected charity (whose patron is HM the Queen), CPRE is often invited to make representations to Government to help frame future policy on countryside matters. Many of our laws on Green Belts, National Parks and the like owe much to the impact of CPRE.

IN KENT

CPRE's Kent branch has been one of the fastest growing in recent years. The organisation continuously seeks to increase local membership. CPRE believes that when those individual voices are brought together they can have a powerful effect. Every new member will add strength to the growing voice of the Kent countryside.

WATCHDOGS

CPRE has local volunteer representatives acting as countryside watchdogs in most parts of Kent. Through the branch offices at Wye, CPRE (Kent) liases with the KCC and District Planning Departments to ensure that concerns for the countryside are taken into account when strategic, county-wide plans are being formulated, such as the Kent Structure Plan, and during the drafting of local plans for each town.

The branch provides representatives, when necessary, during major Public Inquiries to counter the more damaging arguments of development interests.

Members receive regular newsletters, plus the Countryside Campaigner – a magazine covering the pressures on English countryside as a whole.

Full details are available from
CPRE (Kent Branch)
Coldharbour Farm, Wye
Ashford, Kent TN25 5DE

ILLUSTRATION: LESLIE C BENENSON RE

PUCK'S SONG
Rudyard Kipling

See you the dimpled track that runs,
    All hollow through the wheat?
O that was where they hauled the guns
    that smote King Philip's fleet.

See you our little mill that clacks,
    So busy by the brook?
She has ground her corn and paid her tax
    Ever since Domesday Book.

See you the stilly woods of oak,
    And the dread ditch beside?
O that was where the Saxons broke,
    On the day that Harold died.

See you the windy levels spread
    About the gates of Rye?
O that was where the Northmen fled,
    When Alfred's ships came by.

See you our pastures wide and lone,
    Where the red oxen browse?
O there was a city thronged and known,
    Ere London boasted a house.

And see you, after rain, the trace
    Of mound and ditch and wall?
O that was a legion's camping place,
    When Caesar sailed from Gaul.

And see you the marks that show and fade,
    Like shadows on the Downs?
O they are the lines the Flint Men made
    To guard their wondrous'towns.

Trackway and camp and city lost,
    Salt Marsh where now is corn;
Old Wars, old Peace, old Arts that cease,
    And so was England born!

She is not any common Earth,
    Water or wood or air,
But Merlin's isle of Gramarye,
    Where you and I will fare.

Reg. Charity No. 233179

ENGLAND'S COUNTRYSIDE IS ALIVE, WITH ALL ITS INTRICACY, VARIETY AND MAGIC. THIS IS NOT BY CHANCE, BUT BECAUSE GENERATION AFTER GENERATION HAS DEFENDED IT. USING REASONED ARGUMENT CPRE LEADS THAT DEFENCE, QUIETLY AND EFFECTIVELY PUTTING THE CASE FOR THE COUNTRYSIDE WHEREVER DECISIONS AFFECTING ITS FUTURE ARE MADE. IF YOU LOVE THE COUNTRYSIDE, PLEASE JOIN US.

------✂-------------------------------------

YES, I would like to join CPRE. *I ENCLOSE*
☐ £12 (individual)   ☐ £16 (joint)   ☐ £350 (life) And/or ☐£_____ (donation)
I am paying the total of £ _____ by ☐ Cheque/PO (payable to CPRE)
☐ Access/Visa No. ⎢ ⎢ ⎢ ⎢ ⎢ ⎢ ⎢ ⎢ ⎢ ⎢ ⎢ ⎢ ⎢ ⎢ ⎢ ⎢ ⎢ *Expiry date* ____/____
Cardholder's signature _____
PLEASE PRINT
Name(s) _____
Address _____
                                        Postcode _____

PLEASE POST TO COUNCIL FOR THE PROTECTION OF RURAL ENGLAND (CPRE)
FREEPOST, GOLDTHORPE, ROTHERHAM S63 9BR

930

KENT TRUST FOR NATURE CONSERVATION

If you want to support Kent's countryside in a more "down-to-earth" way, then the Kent Trust for Nature Conservation provides many opportunities for practical conservation work. The Trust's Green Teams meet, mainly on Sundays, to carry out a variety of nature reserve tasks: including pond management, the maintenance of pathways and glades, scrub clearing, coppicing, hedgelaying and fencing.

ADVISORY ROLE

The Kent Trust is the county's arm of RSNC (the Wildlife Trust's partnership) a national organisation with over a quarter of a million members.

Across the county, the Trust continuously surveys and monitors threatened wildlife habitats and lobbies hard to protect them.

It also provides advice for both landowners and local authorities on many aspects of conservation.

NATURE RESERVES

A crucial role is the acquisition and management of many sites of special wildlife interest in Kent. To date, the Trust owns and manages well over 4,000 acres of Kent's countryside, often in the most sensitive areas.

Trust reserves include a wide variety of habitats, from fens and reservoirs to woods and areas of downland – including some quite unusual ones – such as the bat habitat in Westerham Mines.

EDUCATIONAL

And the practical is well complemented by the educational. The Trust operates a full programme of walks and talks, through its 9 local groups. Staff work closely with schools and provide a wide range of resource material (including a good selection of leaflets on wildlife and conservation) for teachers and students.

For youngsters, the Trust's WATCH provides an excellent grounding for junior naturalists.

The Trust manages nature reserves and special wildlife areas across the county.

VISITOR CENTRES

The Trust has several visitor centres – Bough Beech in the West, Reculver Country Park in the East and Oare Marshes in the North. The latest at Tyland Barn, Maidstone, is well worth a visit.

For anyone with an interest in conserving Kent's wildlife then the Kent Trust for Nature Conservation is well worth supporting. Full details are available from:

Kent Trust for Nature Conservation,
Tyland Barn,
Chatham Road,
Sandling,
Maidstone ME14 3BD.

As a member, you will receive a guide to KT nature reserves with maps and detailed information on each site, regular magazines including Kent Wildlife Focus, the RSNC's colourful Natural World, and details of local group meetings.

But mostly you will know that you are supporting in a very effective way the conservation of Kent's wildlife.

A DIRECT LINE TO YOUR LOCAL NEIGHBOURHOOD GROUP

KENT FEDERATION OF AMENITY SOCIETIES

The KFAS acts as an umbrella organisation for the vast majority of Kent's 100 or more local amenity societies. Its members are organisations rather than individuals. The Federation will be able to put you in contact with your nearest local organisation.

The KFAS publishes a newsletter with the telling title KENT MATTERS and holds excellent conferences to which the Association invites many of the county's top planners to discuss face-to-face with society representatives the policies which affect and concern their organisations.

You can contact the Kent Federation through:

The Secretary, KFAS,
Clowes House,
Radfall Hill,
Chestfield,
Kent CT5 3ET

RANDOM CONCLUSIONS

Constant change is here to stay. However, you wish to put it the one thing that isn't going to change is man's quest for change.

After all change is never dull. But the scale of some of the changes foisted on our county, and the pace at which they are taking place are not entirely locally-generated, and therefore may, initially at least, seem unwelcome.

That longstanding services have needed to close deserves some comment: schools after close on a century are suddenly unviable, a Maidstone bus company after nearly 50 years, a Folkestone ferry service after 150 years, landscapes which have endured since time immemorial – altered forever. These changes are hardly cosmetic. Many of the changes in Kent have been "large-scale and rapid". Could there have been a similar two/three year period of change in the county's history?

CLIMATE OF OPINION

While the intention of this collection has been to create a coordinated picture, it is on the whole made up of the photographs, the ideas – often the concerns – of many individuals.

If a pattern has emerged, then it could just represent the general climate of opinion. Planners and politicians please note.

DARLING BUDS

In some Kentish villages the "Darling Buds" lifestyle was still around in the seventies – only to be swept aside during the galloping eighties. And yet from the vast audience ratings to the TV series based on the books, there seems little doubt that this quieter, simpler lifestyle is so valued by the general public. Planners and politicans, please note.

NIMBYs

Let's for a moment sidetrack to that term of derision, *NIMBY*, (Not In My Back Yard) ranged at objectors by house building/transport pressure groups and even by a one-time Secretary of State for the Environment. Most people we've met in the course of compiling this book are anything but motivated by their own self-interest. A lot of the photographs are taken of parts of Kent by photographers from a different area. They are concerned for what is happening to the county as a whole. It is just as upsetting to see the bulldozers on the White Cliffs as it is in one's own backyard.

CREEPING CHANGE

Change seems to creep up on us. The photograph below is not very old – from the latter half of the eighties. And yet today, it feels like the M25 has been around for ages.

Continued page 127

CONTINUE TO PHOTOGRAPH
THE CHANGING FACE OF KENT

Although there have been so many changes occurring in the past couple of years, 1992 represents only the start of things to come for Kent.

The Channel Tunnel rail link, new road schemes and expanded towns are planned for the rest of this decade.

Let this book be less a coffee-table curiosity, more a call-to-action. We should like you to continue to send us photographs of any scene in the county that, for good or bad, is facing change. As publishers, we are happy to act as a focus for the collection and will in turn make your photos available to any interested environmental/historical group which can make use of examples of contemporary change. We shall also endeavour to publish the most appropriate contributions in a future book.

DO MY PHOTOGRAPHS NEED TO BE VERY "PROFESSIONAL"?

No. Subject matter is more important. It doesn't matter if you do not have the best camera money can buy; many of the photographs herein were taken on compacts. What does matter is that scenes are captured on camera before they are lost. Some of your work could represent the last opportunity many of us will have to view that particular Kentish scene and provide a valuable historical record for future generations.

SHOULD I USE BLACK/WHITE FILM?

Due to the high cost of colour printing (this may change in future) we mainly publish in black and white. If you can send us the photo in black and white, all well and good. But it isn't essential. Many of the examples in this book were submitted in colour, which is generally so much easier to have processed. What we do ask is that, if possible, you send us a larger print, 7in × 5in or above (most high street processors now provide the larger sizes) rather than an enprint, and that it is understood that we have your permission to publish the photograph and to pass it on to other environmental/historical groups for them to use non-commercially.

We shall endeavour to inform all photographers of any future publication in which their work may appear.

Remember, your photograph may represent one of the last opportunities any of us may have of viewing that particular Kentish scene.

SPOTTING CHANGE BEFORE IT HAPPENS

Perhaps the best photograph depicting change shows a scene/building before it is developed. But this is not always possible and inevitably many of the photographs are recorded later with the bulldozers already in. We are always very happy to receive these. However, there are ways in which you can be aware of change before it actually happens.

Most major developments are outlined many months in advance in your local newspapers. Locally, your council will often supply lists of proposals to change a building or a tract of nearby countryside; and most towns will soon be covered by a Local Plan, available from your District Council offices showing proposed future changes in land-use with some idea of the timescales involved.

Organisations such as the CPRE (Coldharbour Farm, Amage Road, Wye, Ashford, Kent TN25 5DE) continuously monitor all developments which might affect the Kent landscape. The KCC and Department of Transport publish books of road schemes planned for Kent.

Once you are aware of a proposal, don't wait, take a photograph as soon as convenient. A little forward planning may be necessary. Some shots are best taken at a particular time of day when the sun is in the right place. But generally it is better to take the photograph on the first available opportunity. Especially in "boom" times, redevelopment can take place very soon after planning permission is granted.

So don't delay. You can send us your photographs at any time. Further publications will be considered, not to any specific deadline, but every two years or so, depending upon the number of examples received.

ONCE QUIET SPOTS CLOSE TO TOWN

Continued from page 125

As the Gateway to Europe, Kent could see a dramatic increase in air and road traffic during the nineties.

With all the new road and rail schemes put forward, with new by-passes skirting many of our towns, we are beginning to wonder if soon there will be any quiet spots at all left in Kent close to our main towns. Hence the Challenge on page 35.

We're looking for the kind of places on the edge of town most of us grew up knowing. Places common everywhere, just a handful of years ago.

If you live in a reasonably-sized Kentish town, with say a population of 10,000 plus, then we should like to invite you to nominate a quiet beauty spot, still free from traffic and other disturbances close-by.

It should:

– be a quiet spot, free from all traffic
– be close to town, say within 10 minutes stroll from home
– have some point of attraction to locals, such as a river, a viewpoint or similar
– not be under threat from any foreseen development
– be described sufficiently clearly

Write your entry, with a description of how to find it (ordnance survey references or a sketch map if possible – but not essential) on a postcard, together with your name and address. Post it to:

Heathrow Publications
Palace Business Estate
Maidstone
ME15 9XU

We will place all nominations "in the hat", draw half a dozen and from them award a prize to the one we judge to be the best example of a quiet spot close to town.

The challenge is open to all owners of this book. Staple the corner coupon below to your postcard as proof of purchase and send to us before December 1993. A total prize of £250 will be awarded to the winner; made up of £125 to yourself plus £125 to any environmental charity of your choosing. Best of luck.

So what? Shouldn't we have an M25? Isn't arguing against motorways arguing away the jobs of thousands of construction workers?

Not necessarily. We could logically argue for more public finances for the construction industry – so that the industry could match the undoubted technical quality of its projects with a new environmental quality – with more tunnels, different routes giving less destruction in sensitive areas, more steps to reduce traffic noise and the like. Similarly in our towns, let's have a presumption for good architecture, not developments "thrown up to meet a price."

Everyone likes their car. But, in encouraging a car-orientated society we do not only risk altering our environment. Social patterns change.

People no longer work and shop where they live. We are surely undermining the community feel to our towns and villages. This year the closure of the village shop, next year what?

How long will it take for Kent to lose its unique character? Perhaps it will take on a more European face. Which leads us to one final irony on the Channel Tunnel. The very same British politicians who in the mid-eighties forced through the hybrid bill for this most concrete symbol of Britain's new ties with Europe seem now almost to a man (and a woman) our leading Euro-sceptics.

From the Garden of England to Europe's Gateway – how far along this path will we 'progress'? Whatever the answer, in the three short years covered by this book the process has surely begun.

127

**Do you like the scale and
pace of progress in Kent today?
Let your planners and politicians know!**